GOODNIGHT, BOONE

by Yozette "Yogi" Collins & Marlis Jennings

illustrations by Ania Ziolkowski

AllStar
P R E S S

In the great log cabin beneath

some trees...

There is a bowl full of candy and a pair of skis
A dog named Champ at the hearth of stone...

...and Grandfather Mountain with its profile so strong

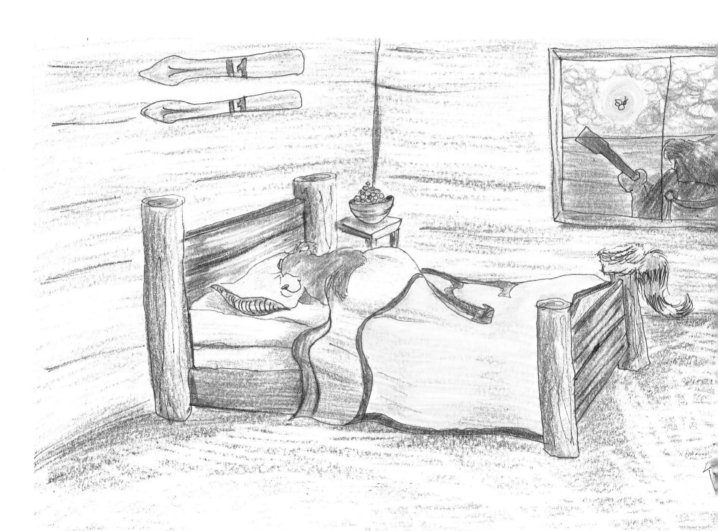

Dad on the porch softly playing a tune
as I drift to sleep tucked in bed in my room

Goodnight, Grandfather

Goodnight, Boone

Goodnight Daddy strumming a tune

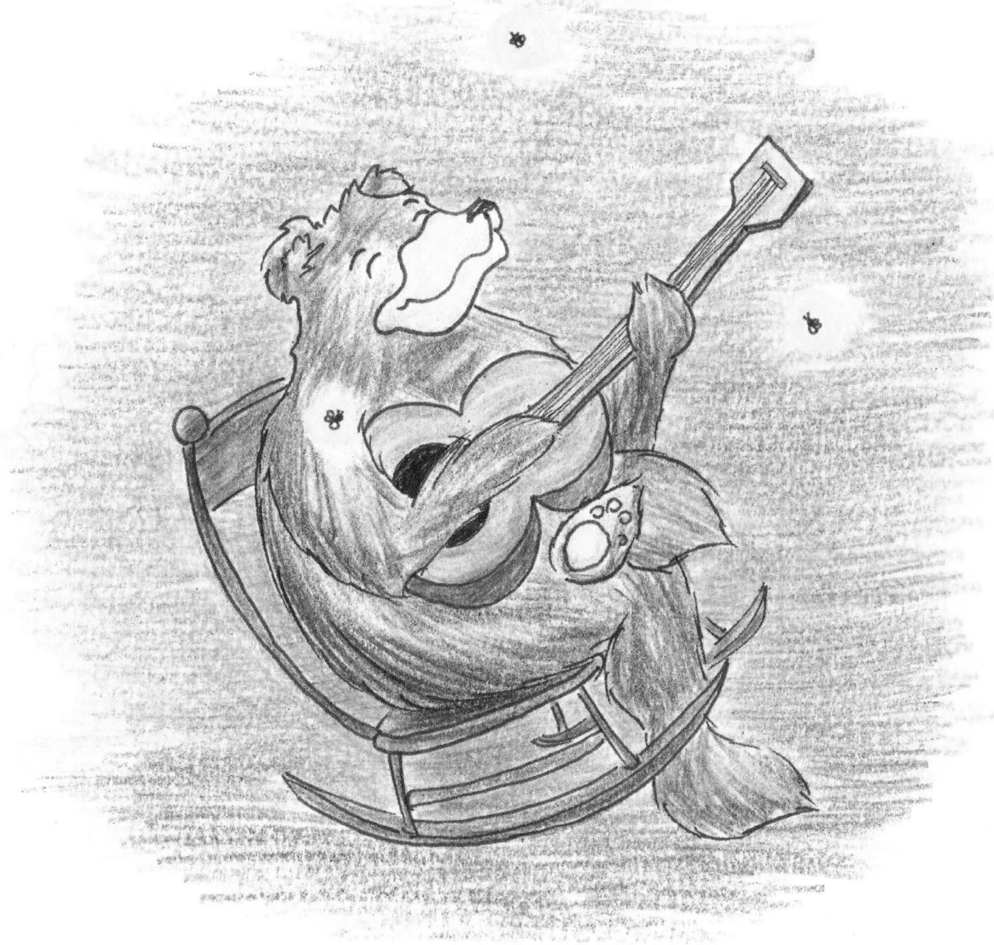

Goodnight candy that came from Mast

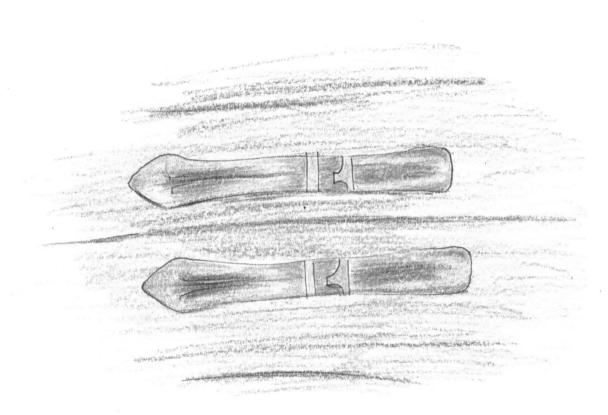

Goodnight skis that go so fast

Goodnight trees...

Goodnight leaves...

Goodnight firewood stacked under the eaves

Goodnight, Champ...

...and goodnight boots

Goodnight train that sings toot-toot

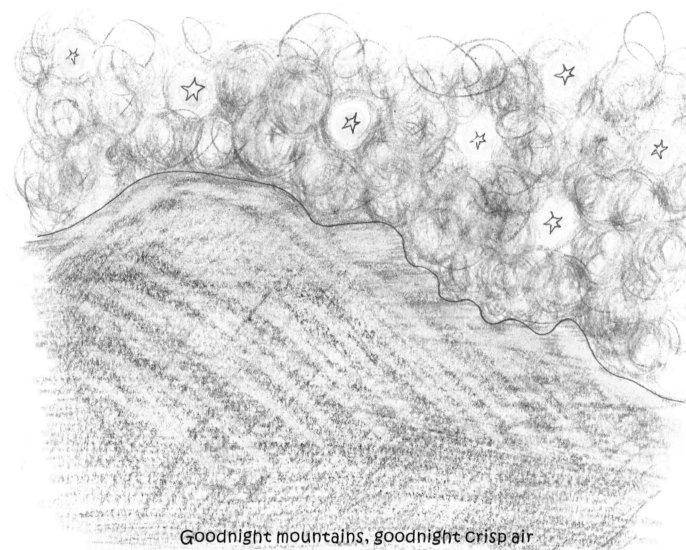

Goodnight mountains, goodnight crisp air

Goodnight beauty...everywhere

CPSIA information can be obtained
at www.ICGtesting.com
Printed in the USA
LVIC04n0805020616
490886LV00003B/9

* 9 7 8 1 9 3 7 3 7 6 1 8 5 *